DOGS
DOGS
DOGS

DOGS DOGS DOGS

A COLLECTION OF GREAT DOG CARTOONS

EDITED BY S. GROSS

BARNES
&NOBLE
BOOKS
NEW YORK

Some of the cartoons in this collection have appeared in the following periodicals and are reprinted by permission of the authors: *American Health, Audubon, Boston Phoenix, Chicago Magazine, Christian Science Monitor, Diversion, Fantasy and Science Fiction, Good Housekeeping, Household, Ladies' Home Journal, In the Know, Look, National Lampoon, The New York Times, Psychology Today, Saturday Evening Post, Saturday Review, Scouting, This Week, Trial Diplomacy Journal, Wilson Library Bulletin, Woman's World.*

Grateful acknowledgment is made for permission to reprint:

The cartoon by Lo Linkert on page 56 from *Golf Digest.* Copyright © 1985 by Golf Digest/Tennis, Inc. Reprinted by permission of the author and *Golf Digest.*

The cartoon by Joseph Mirachi on page 10 from *Sports Illustrated.* Copyright © 1956 Time Inc.

The cartoon by Brian Savage on page 62 from *OMNI.* Copyright © 1981 by Omni International Limited. Reprinted courtesy of *OMNI* magazine.

Cartoons copyrighted by *The New Yorker* are indicated throughout the book.

1997 Barnes & Noble Books

ISBN 0-7607-0544-5

Printed and bound in the United States of America

98 99 00 01 M 9 8 7 6 5 4 3 2

RRDH

DOGS
DOGS
DOGS

"And *this,* I presume, is Fluffy?"

"Of course he said 'Arf.' What did you expect
his first word to be?"

WILLIAM MAUL

ED FISHER

"It's for you."

"Tough work, owning a dog."

LIZA DONNELLY

"Well, I can see there *are* differences to work out, but basically,
I feel, you still have a sound dog-and-little-old-lady relationship."

JARED LEE

"Oh, Elizabeth! I didn't recognize you."

ED FRASCINO

"You really *are* man's best friend."

JERRY MARCUS

"Your exact words, as I recall, were: 'Her puppies
will sell like hotcakes!' "

DONALD OREHEK

BERNARD SCHOENBAUM

"He eats from the garbage, he could sleep in the garage,
and his wine only costs 98 cents a bottle.
Oh please, daddy, please can we keep him?"

TIM HAGGERTY

"I hope we're not intruding, but Chester picked up a trail
he couldn't let go of."

PETER STEINER

LEO CULLUM

9

"Maybe it's the propylene glycol you don't go for."
JOE MIRACHI

"Next!"

VAHAN SHIRVANIAN

"Unfortunately, I took him into one of those 'if you break it you bought it' places."

ANDY WYATT

BILL WOODMAN

"OK, Binkie. You can let go of the slippers now."

"Miss Olmstead, may we have another doggie treat?"

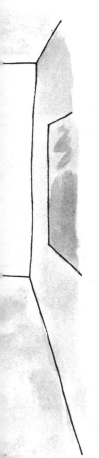

WILLIAM MAUL

JACK ZIEGLER

15

BILL WOODMAN

"Why, no, I didn't see any fox go past here."

"Before we begin the board meeting, which one of you is going
to take this one last puppy off my hands?"

PETER STEINER

"We don't look much alike, but have you noticed that
our personalities are identical?"

ED FRASCINO

gerberg
MORT GERBERG

CATHARINE O'NEILL

"Oh, it's quite all right to discuss him by name; Timmy's the kind of dog
who doesn't mind being referred to in the third person."

MORT GERBERG

"He's just warming it up for me."

ORLANDO BUSINO

20

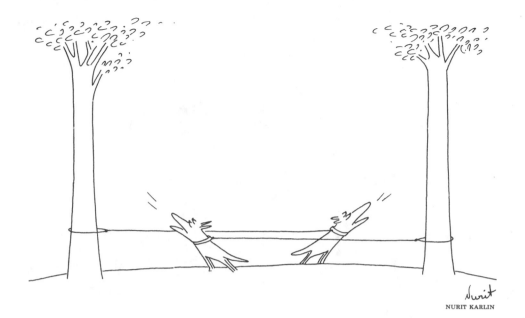

NURIT KARLIN

TIM HAGGERTY

S. GROSS

22

"On TV they run over to it and wag their tails." SIDNEY HARRIS

"After ten years you're allowed to have a pet."

JOHN CALDWELL

"Next time just bring the slippers. I'll get the pipe myself!"

AARON BACALL

"I don't take you out enough."

BORIS DRUCKER

VAHAN SHIRVANIAN

"Sweetheart, could you maybe include the dog?"

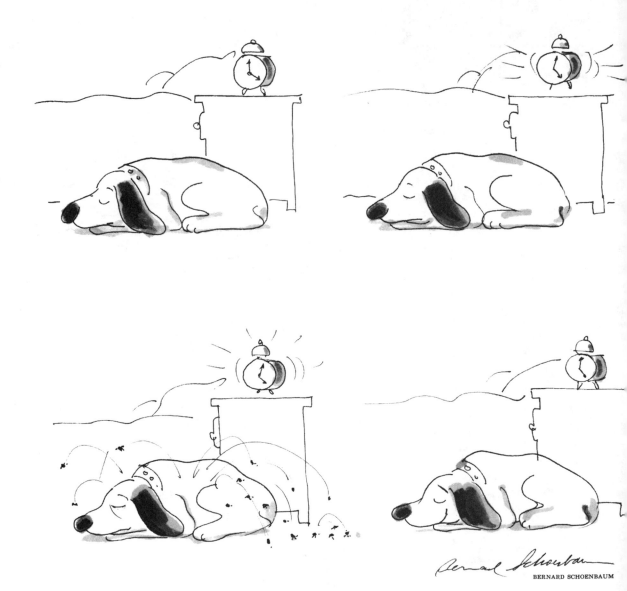

BERNARD SCHOENBAUM

"Inflation, baby."

CHARLES SAUERS

"See? It's not as if you were the only one."

GAHAN WILSON
© 1981 The New Yorker Magazine, Inc.

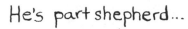

DAVID SIPRESS

"What did you say to him?"

ED FRASCINO

"They all want doggie bags!"

JERRY MARCUS

"Now play dead."

"There's a reply to your ad for a companion."

DONALD OREHEK

"Due to the sudden illness of one of our stars, the role of Clancy
will be essayed by yours truly."

BRIAN SAVAGE

A MAN AND
HIS DOG

CBarsotti

"From the left: Jeremiah Brisco III, Anthony Cortland
of Sutherland Haven, Terhune Hempstead of Intervale-Hempstead,
Sir Fairmont Starspray of Griscombshire, Ferguson Fentlow
of Fairlea, and, of course, Al."

"Is wittle Pookah hungwy?"

JACK ZIEGLER

"I taught him to talk. . . . You teach him to shut up."

ANDY WYATT

MIKE TWOHY

"A kiss will break the enchantment and people will call me Prince again."

"Thanks."

ORLANDO BUSINO

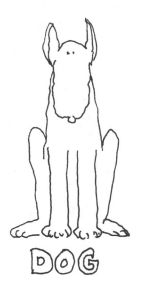

DOG   DOGGIE   DAWG

THOMAS CHENEY

"You mustn't wake him, Charles. He's walking in his sleep."

M. K. BROWN

1.

2.

3.

4.

5.

6. ▶

7.

8.

9.

"No, no, Sparky. Stay!"

BUD GRACE

"I suppose you know you're spoiling that dog."

"I'm getting worried, doc—he's been playing dead
for two weeks now."

RICHARD ORLIN

SIPRESS
DAVID SIPRESS

44

"Hey, down in front!"

ARNIE LEVIN

CALLAHAN

"Just how big does he get?"

"Wellington is much improved with the loving care of those
three great physicians, *nature, time,* and *patience,* Lucille,
but the pit bull is six bricks short of a full load."

GEORGE BOOTH

"I've come for your fleas."

JOHN CALDWELL

"Everyone should have, at least in spirit,
an enthusiastic dog."

LIZA DONNELLY

DAVID PASCAL

VAHAN SHIRVANIAN

"He doesn't bite, but there are zillions of germs
on his tongue."

REX MAY (BALOO)

"Who would've dreamed he'd be this jealous over a new baby?"

WILLIAM MAUL

OLD DOG / NEW TRICK

MICK STEVENS

"I had that nightmare again. The one where I'm walking
down the street stark naked."

ED FRASCINO

FELIPE GALINDO (FEGGO)

"Poor thing! He just seems to *know* that something terrible
is happening in Afghanistan!"

ED FISHER

TONY ROSA

"... and yet, she did not think only of herself. She always
considered the wishes of others. No matter how depressed
she was, no matter how tired she was, if you threw
a stick and told her to 'fetch' ..."

SIDNEY HARRIS

"He eats every five minutes on the fifth minute."

BORIS DRUCKER

CHARLES ADDAMS

LO LINKERT

"Of course you don't notice any difference, sir—
I taught him to obey *me!*"

JARED LEE

"Cut that out!"

PHIL INTERLANDI

JOSEPH FARRIS

"Now watch this. Sit!"

MICHAEL CRAWFORD

"Yes, it's true. You were adopted."

HENRY MARTIN

"We're trying to teach him not to jump up on people."

LEO CULLUM

"So you have killed. Any qualms about it?"

TIM HAGGERTY

BERNARD SCHOENBAUM

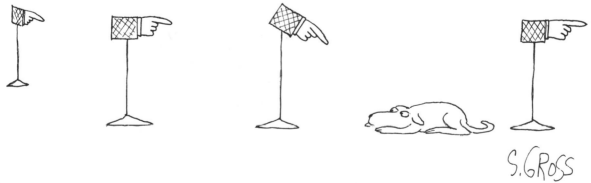

S. GROSS

BRIAN SAVAGE
Reprinted courtesy *OMNI* magazine © 1981.

CHOMP! CHOMP! CHOMP!

BOOTH '85

GEORGE BOOTH

"You're allergic to . . ."

SIDNEY HARRIS

"I'll prove it wasn't Tramp. . . . Here boy, here boy . . . !"

DONALD OREHEK

1.

2.

3.

4.

ZIEGLER

JACK ZIEGLER

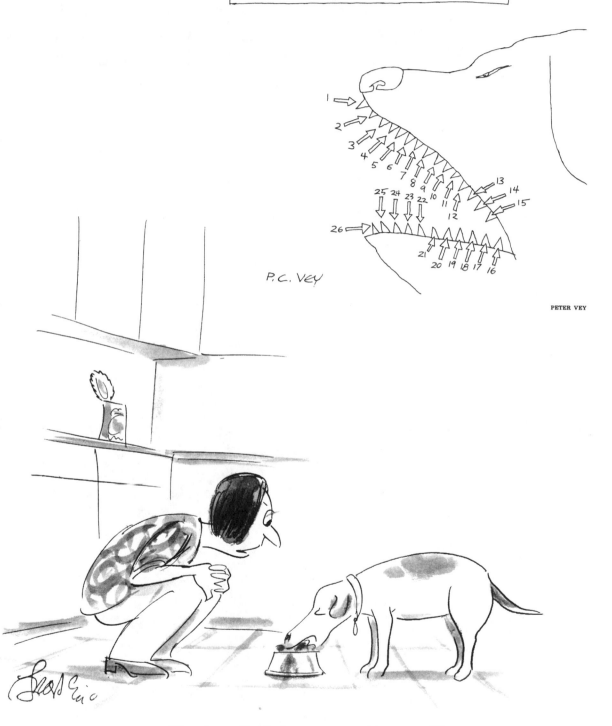

"How do you like it when someone watches *you* eat?"

ED FRASCINO

"Will you come on? I was kidding!"

"That happens to be *my* chair!"

MORT GERBERG

LIZA DONNELLY

U.S. POST OFFICE

VAHAN SHIRVANIAN

DR. PLAUT
VETERINARIAN

"I sure hope you can do that right. I'm tired of having to find
a new vet after every shot."

ORLANDO BUSINO

MORT GERBERG

W. MILLER
© 1982 The New Yorker Magazine, Inc.

"Now you know which one to push, Peppy. Push 'one.'"

BILL WOODMAN

DONALD OREHEK

JOHN JONIK

"Thank God we only do this once a month."

BUD GRACE

PETER PORGES

CATHARINE O'NEILL

"He's looking right at you, too. I hope you're proud of yourself
for saving eight cents on that brand."

FRANK MODELL
© 1979 The New Yorker Magazine, Inc.

"It doesn't just say 'dog'—it says '*hot* dog'!"

AL ROSS

VAHAN SHIRVANIAN

"It's heavy panting. It must be for you."

MORT GERBERG

"These are his sunset years."

ROBERT WEBER

"Give me a call when he gets over that lisp."

JERRY MARCUS

Zack Brillard and Live-In Companion

ROBERT MANKOFF

ARNIE LEVIN

"For heaven's sake, say 'please.'"

BERNARD SCHOENBAUM

"Go fetch."

TIM HAGGERTY

"Excuse me, Reverend. Your pup runneth over."

ANDY WYATT

"Valerie at Puppy Preen created the cut especially for her."

ED FRASCINO

BOOTH.
GEORGE BOOTH
© 1980 The New Yorker Magazine, Inc.

". . . except ours had a shorter tail and slightly longer ears."

BARNEY TOBEY

WILLIAM MAUL

FRANK MODELL
© 1973 The New Yorker Magazine, Inc.

"What about me? When do I get breakfast in bed?"

LEO CULLUM

DAVID JACOBSON

S. GROSS

"He's very much involved with the moon."

BORIS DRUCKER
© 1980 The New Yorker Magazine, Inc.

BRIAN SAVAGE

ED ARNO

NAME THAT COAST!

CHECK ONE:

A) GOLDEN RETRIEVER ☐
B) COLLIE ☐
C) BEAGLE ☐
D) DALMATIAN ☐
E) COCKER SPANIEL ☐

MICHAEL CRAWFORD

"Good boy!"

ORLANDO BUSINO

JACK ZIEGLER

BILL WOODMAN

"Isn't it amazing how people look like their dogs!"

JOHN CALLAHAN

"Of course you can serve him. He's 3½. That's way over 21 in human terms."

SIDNEY HARRIS